The Silent Guardians

Protecting Democracy During the WWII Era

Written by

Mcbillz Monroe

asserts the author's ownership of this Book and specifies that no part of the book may be reproduced without permission from the publisher.

TABLE OF CONTENTS

INTRODUCTION

In the darkest days of World War II, a battle raged not just on foreign soil but within the heart of America itself. This wasn't a fight marked by bombs or bullets, but by the quiet, determined actions of individuals who saw the threat to democracy and acted. They were not the soldiers we read about in history books, but everyday citizens and public servants who understood the dire stakes and rose to meet them.

Picture this: America in the early 1940s, a nation divided in its stance on the war unfolding in Europe. Isolationists argued vehemently to keep the United States out of the conflict, while interventionists saw the writing on the wall and pushed for action. Amidst this turmoil, a

more insidious threat emerged—
a small but dangerous faction of
far-right plotters, eager to steer
America towards an alliance
with the Nazis.

These plotters weren't just
random extremists; they
included influential figures with
access to power and resources.
They worked to sway public
opinion, infiltrate government
positions, and undermine the

nation's democratic foundations. They saw an opportunity in the chaos of war and aimed to exploit it for their gain.

Enter the silent guardians. They were a mix of public officials, journalists, lawyers, and activists, each driven by a profound sense of duty to protect their country. Their weapons were not guns, but pens and papers, legal briefs, and the sheer force of their conviction. They operated in shadows, often without the recognition or support they deserved, but their impact was undeniable.

One such figure was a young lawyer named Tom Clark, who would later become the Attorney General. In the early days of the war, Clark saw the rising tide of fascism and took it upon himself to root out subversive elements within the government. He worked tirelessly, sometimes bending the rules but always with the aim of preserving the democratic process.

Then there was the journalist Dorothy Thompson, one of the few who sounded the alarm about the Nazi threat long before it became common knowledge.

Thompson used her platform to expose the activities of Nazi sympathizers in America, facing backlash and censorship but never backing down. Her fearless reporting brought to light the dangers that many preferred to ignore.

At the same time, inside the halls of power, a group of senators led by Robert Wagner and his colleagues worked behind the scenes to craft legislation that would safeguard civil liberties while allowing for the prosecution of those who sought to undermine the government. They navigated a delicate balance, aware that overreach could lead to the very tyranny they were fighting against.

These efforts were not without controversy. Accusations of overreach and fear-mongering flew from all sides. The silent guardians walked a tightrope, balancing the need for security with the imperative to maintain the freedoms that defined their nation. They faced opposition from those who believed they were too harsh, as well as from those who felt they were not doing enough.

As the war progressed, the stakes only grew higher. The

Pearl Harbor attack in 1941 galvanized the nation, but it also heightened the internal threats. Japanese Americans were unjustly interned, a dark chapter in American history that some of these guardians tried to prevent, though often unsuccessfully. This period tested the very fabric of American society, forcing it to confront its values and the lengths it would go to protect them.

In the shadows, far-right conspiracies continued to brew. Groups like the German American Bund, which held rallies supporting Hitler, and other extremist organizations, remained a constant threat. The silent guardians had to be vigilant, adapting their strategies as the enemy evolved. They infiltrated these groups, gathered intelligence, and worked to dismantle their networks from within.

Their victories were often small and unheralded. A disrupted rally here, a foiled plot there. But each success was a step towards ensuring that the principles of democracy endured. They laid the groundwork for the eventual Allied victory, not just in Europe but in the ideological battle that defined the era. These efforts culminated in the war's end, but the lessons learned carried forward. The silent guardians' legacy lived on in the institutions they strengthened and the precedents they set. They showed that democracy requires constant vigilance, that the fight to protect it never truly ends.

Looking back, it's clear that their actions, though perhaps unseen and uncelebrated at the time, were essential. They operated in a time of great uncertainty, yet their resolve never wavered. Their story is one of courage and conviction, a testament to the power of individuals to make a difference, even in the face of overwhelming odds.

In telling this story, we honor not just their memory but the ideals they fought to protect. It's a reminder that democracy is not a given, but a fragile system that requires our unwavering dedication. The silent guardians of WWII taught us that true patriotism lies in the quiet, determined actions that defend the freedoms we hold dear, actions that are as vital today as they were then.

CHAPTER 1: THE EARLY THREAT

The 1930s saw the rise of fascism across Europe, and even across the pond in America, a dangerous ideology began to seep into the fringes of society. As Hitler tightened his grip on Germany, sympathizers in the United States began to emerge, hoping to replicate his authoritarian regime. This was no mere ideological dalliance; these were serious, well-funded efforts to undermine American democracy from within.

Groups like the German American Bund sprang up, blatantly parading their admiration for the Führer. Led by Fritz Kuhn, a naturalized American citizen of German descent, the Bund wasn't just a social club. It hosted rallies, complete with swastikas and anti-Semitic rhetoric, aimed at recruiting American citizens to the Nazi cause. The sight of brown-shirted marchers on American streets, zealously saluting and spouting hateful propaganda, was a chilling reminder of the growing threat.

These weren't isolated incidents. Wealthy industrialists, like Henry Ford, openly expressed their anti-Semitic views, using their influence and money to spread fascist ideologies. Newspapers, pamphlets, and even radio broadcasts carried their messages, reaching into American homes and hearts. The isolationist sentiment in America, still reeling from the Great Depression and wary of another overseas conflict, created fertile ground for these dangerous ideas to take root.

Political figures, too, were not immune. Senator Burton Wheeler of Montana, a staunch isolationist, criticized Roosevelt's foreign policy, arguing vehemently against any involvement in the European war. Charles Lindbergh, a national hero for his solo transatlantic flight, became a vocal advocate for America First, a movement that sought to keep the U.S. out of the conflict. His speeches often carried a whiff of sympathy for Hitler, masked by his calls for American neutrality.

Amidst this backdrop, President Franklin D. Roosevelt faced immense pressure. Balancing the need to prepare the nation for the possibility of war while countering the rising tide of fascism within was no easy task. The FBI, under J. Edgar Hoover, ramped up surveillance of suspected Nazi sympathizers, infiltrating meetings and tracking their activities. Hoover, known for his obsession with subversives, directed his agents to leave no stone unturned.

It wasn't just the federal government taking action. Local law enforcement and private citizens began to organize against the growing threat.

Groups like the Non-Sectarian Anti-Nazi League, led by Jewish activist Samuel Untermyer, launched campaigns to boycott German goods and expose Nazi activities in America. Their efforts shone a light on the dark corners where fascism tried to hide.

Public sentiment was a battleground in itself. Propaganda played a crucial role, with both sides vying to win the hearts and minds of the American people. Films, posters, and newsreels depicted the stark realities of Nazi aggression and the moral imperative to resist it. The government's Office of War Information crafted messages that underscored the dangers of fascism, not just abroad but at home.

In the cultural arena, authors, playwrights, and artists used their platforms to rally against fascism. Sinclair Lewis's novel "It Can't Happen Here" imagined a dystopian America under a fascist regime, serving as a stark warning of what could be. The play "Watch on the Rhine" by Lillian Hellman brought the threat to the stage, dramatizing the conflict between democracy and fascism.

Educational institutions also became a front in this ideological battle. Universities held debates and lectures on the perils of fascism, with professors like Franz Boas and John Dewey speaking out against the encroaching threat. Student groups, often dismissed as naive or overly idealistic, organized protests and distributed literature to counter fascist propaganda.

Despite these efforts, the threat continued to grow. The infamous rally at Madison Square Garden in 1939, organized by the German American Bund, drew 20,000 supporters, filling the iconic venue with banners depicting George Washington surrounded by swastikas. Outside, tens of thousands of protestors clashed with police, a stark illustration of the nation's division.

These early years were marked by a sense of urgency and frustration. While many Americans remained blissfully unaware or willfully ignorant of the dangers, those in the know felt the weight of their responsibility. They worked tirelessly, often in secret, to counteract the spread of fascism. Their methods varied, from legal action and public shaming to direct confrontation and sabotage.

The government's crackdown intensified as the war in Europe escalated. The Smith Act of 1940 made it illegal to advocate for the violent overthrow of the government, targeting Nazi sympathizers and other subversive groups. This legislation, while controversial, gave law enforcement the tools they needed to disrupt these dangerous networks.

As America moved closer to entering the war, the internal threat of fascism began to wane, but it never disappeared entirely. The legacy of these early efforts laid the groundwork for a more vigilant society, one that recognized the importance of safeguarding democracy from within as well as from without.

The early threat of fascism in America was a test of the nation's resolve and values. It revealed the vulnerabilities within a democracy, the ease with which dangerous ideologies could take root, and the lengths to which ordinary citizens and officials would go to protect their country. The silent guardians of this era—lawyers, journalists, activists, and government agents—acted with courage and conviction, often at great personal risk.

Their stories remind us that the fight for democracy is never-ending. It requires constant vigilance, a willingness to confront uncomfortable truths, and the bravery to stand against the tide. In the face of growing darkness, these silent guardians became beacons of hope, illuminating the path forward for future generations. Their legacy is one of resilience and determination, a testament to the enduring power of individual action in the defence of freedom.

CHAPTER 2: THE ALLIES WITHIN

In the swirling chaos of World War II, not all threats to democracy were external. Within the United States, a hidden army of loyal Americans worked tirelessly to counteract the insidious rise of fascist sympathizers. These were the allies within, ordinary citizens and officials who understood that the fight for freedom began at home.

In the FBI's headquarters, J. Edgar Hoover sat at the helm, directing operations with his characteristic intensity. Hoover's obsession with rooting out subversives made him the perfect spearhead for this internal battle. His agents infiltrated far-right groups, attending meetings in disguise, gathering intelligence, and meticulously building cases against those who sought to align America with the Axis powers.

Meanwhile, a journalist named Dorothy Thompson wielded her typewriter like a weapon. Once expelled from Germany by Hitler himself, Thompson returned to the U.S. with a fervent mission to expose Nazi sympathizers. Her columns reached millions, pulling no punches as she laid bare the dangers lurking within American society. Thompson's relentless pursuit of truth earned her both admirers and enemies, but she remained undeterred.

In the halls of Congress, Representative Martin Dies Jr. led the House Un-American Activities Committee (HUAC). Though the committee would later gain infamy during the McCarthy era, in the early days of WWII, it focused on genuine threats. Dies and his team hauled suspected Nazi sympathizers before the committee, grilling them under the bright lights and broadcasting their testimonies to the nation. These hearings were a spectacle, designed to unmask those who sought to undermine the American way of life.

Labor unions also became battlegrounds in this ideological war. The American Federation of Labor (AFL) and the Congress of Industrial Organizations (CIO) took strong stances against fascism, recognizing the threat it posed to workers' rights and freedoms. Union leaders like Philip Murray and William Green used their considerable influence to rally workers against Nazi ideology, organizing rallies and strikes to demonstrate their solidarity with the war effort.

Churches and religious leaders, too, joined the fray. The Catholic Church, in particular, took a firm stand against fascism. Clergymen like Father Charles Coughlin initially spread anti-Semitic rhetoric, but a strong backlash from within the Church and the wider community forced him off the air. Other religious leaders used their pulpits to preach messages of unity and resistance, urging their congregations to stand firm against the seductive call of fascism.

The entertainment industry didn't sit idle either. Hollywood, always attuned to the mood of the nation, churned out films that highlighted the dangers of fascism and celebrated democratic values. Directors like Frank Capra created propaganda films for the U.S. government, blending entertainment with powerful messages about the importance of the war effort. Stars like James Stewart and Clark Gable enlisted, using their fame to boost morale and promote patriotic duty.

Academia became another front in this internal war. Universities and colleges hosted debates, lectures, and symposiums on the rise of fascism, drawing on the expertise of historians, political scientists, and philosophers. Professors like Reinhold Niebuhr and John Dewey spoke passionately about the need to defend democracy, inspiring a new generation of students to engage in the struggle.

These efforts weren't without risk. FBI agents faced real danger infiltrating extremist groups, risking exposure and retaliation. Journalists like Thompson received death threats and found themselves targeted by powerful adversaries. Politicians like Dies faced immense pressure from lobbyists and constituents who didn't see the threat as he did. Yet, they pressed on, driven by a shared belief in the necessity of their mission.

Among these allies, the role of ordinary citizens cannot be overstated. Neighbors reported suspicious activities, local business owners refused to serve known sympathizers, and community groups organized to spread awareness and support the war effort. The Civilian Defense organization trained volunteers in air raid precautions, first aid, and even espionage detection, creating a network of vigilant citizens ready to act.

At the grassroots level, women played a particularly vital role. Organizations like the Women's Army Auxiliary Corps (WAAC) and the Women's Airforce

Service Pilots (WASP) allowed women to serve in capacities previously reserved for men, freeing up soldiers for combat roles and proving women's capabilities in defense. These women not only filled critical gaps but also brought a new perspective and energy to the fight against fascism.

Even children were enlisted in the cause. Schools

implemented programs to educate students about the war, encouraging them to collect scrap metal, buy war bonds, and participate in victory gardens. These initiatives fostered a sense of collective responsibility and ensured that the next generation understood the importance of safeguarding democracy.

The war effort saw the collaboration of these diverse

allies, each playing a unique role in protecting the nation from within. Their combined actions created a tapestry of resistance, a network of vigilance that spanned every corner of American society. It was a messy, chaotic, often dangerous endeavor, but it was effective.

The impact of these allies within cannot be understated. They disrupted plots, exposed traitors, and shifted public opinion. They fortified the nation's resolve, reminding Americans that the fight for freedom was not just overseas but right in their own backyard. Their work ensured that when America finally joined the war, it did so with a united front, resilient and ready to face the challenges ahead.

These allies were not just fighting against an ideology; they were fighting for the soul of their nation. They understood that democracy, with all its flaws and complexities, was worth defending. Their legacy is a testament to the power of collective action and the importance of standing up for what is right, even when the enemy is within.

CHAPTER 3: GOVERNMENTAL MEASURES

In the heart of Washington, D.C., the corridors of power buzzed with a new urgency as the Second World War loomed ever closer. The United States government, keenly aware of the threats both abroad and at home, began implementing a series of measures to safeguard the nation. President Franklin D. Roosevelt, a master of navigating turbulent waters, spearheaded these efforts with a blend of charisma and steely determination. His administration recognized that protecting democracy required more than just military might; it demanded a robust, coordinated effort on multiple fronts.

The first major step was the establishment of the Office of War Information (OWI) in 1942. This agency, led by journalist Elmer Davis, had a clear mandate: to disseminate accurate information about the war and counter enemy propaganda. The OWI churned out posters, films, and radio broadcasts designed to boost morale and foster unity. They painted vivid pictures of the stakes, making the war's implications clear to every American citizen. This was not just about defeating the Axis powers; it was about preserving the very fabric of American society.

Simultaneously, the Roosevelt administration saw the need for economic stability. Enter the War Production Board (WPB), created in 1942 to oversee the conversion of peacetime industries to war production. Chaired by Donald Nelson, a former executive of Sears, Roebuck & Co., the WPB marshalled resources with military precision. Factories that once produced consumer goods pivoted to making tanks, planes, and munitions. This economic shift not only ensured a steady supply of war materials but also invigorated the economy, pulling the nation out of the Great Depression.

But the government's measures went beyond propaganda and production. Security within the nation's borders became a top priority. The Smith Act of 1940, officially known as the Alien Registration Act, laid down severe penalties for those advocating the overthrow of the government. It required all noncitizen adults to register with the government, providing fingerprints and detailed personal information. This act, controversial yet effective, was a tool to identify and monitor potential subversives.

Another layer of security came with the creation of the Office of Strategic Services (OSS) in 1942, the precursor to the CIA. Under the leadership of William "Wild

Bill" Donovan, the OSS conducted espionage, gathered intelligence, and executed covert operations. Donovan's operatives, often drawn from the ranks of academics, athletes, and even Hollywood, worked behind enemy lines to sabotage Axis operations and gather crucial information. The OSS's efforts were shrouded in secrecy, but their impact was profound, shaping the intelligence landscape for years to come.

Domestically, the government took steps to ensure the loyalty of its citizens. The Federal Bureau of Investigation (FBI), under the watchful eye of J. Edgar Hoover, ramped up its activities. Hoover, a man of boundless energy and suspicion, directed his agents to infiltrate and dismantle fascist and communist cells within the United States. The FBI's methods were often heavy-handed, involving wiretaps, surveillance, and informants. Yet, these measures were deemed necessary to root out threats to national security.

The government also recognised the importance of maintaining public order and morale. The Civilian Defense program mobilised millions of Americans on the home front. Volunteers donned armbands and helmets, ready to respond to air raids, natural disasters, and other emergencies. This program not only prepared the nation for potential attacks but also fostered a sense of community and shared purpose. Citizens were no longer passive observers; they were active participants in the defense of their country.

Economic measures extended to the financial sector as well. The War Bonds program, launched with much fanfare, encouraged Americans to invest in their country's future. Celebrities and politicians alike promoted war bonds, framing them as both a patriotic duty and a sound investment. The Treasury

Department's efforts paid off handsomely, with millions of Americans purchasing bonds and thus financing the war effort. This influx of funds ensured that the military had the resources needed to sustain its campaigns abroad.

Labour relations, always a contentious issue, saw significant government intervention. The National War

Labor Board (NWLB), established in 1942, aimed to prevent strikes and ensure industrial peace. Chaired by William Hammatt Davis, the NWLB mediated disputes between workers and employers, arbitrating issues of wages, hours, and working conditions. This intervention was crucial in maintaining uninterrupted production, as labour unrest could have dire consequences for the war effort.

Civil liberties, however, faced severe tests. The internment of Japanese Americans, authorised by Executive Order 9066, stands as one of the darkest chapters of this period. Over 120,000 individuals of Japanese descent, many of them U.S. citizens, were forcibly relocated to internment camps. The government justified this action as a necessary security measure, but it was driven by fear and prejudice. The internment left a lasting scar, a stark reminder of the fragility of civil rights in times of crisis.

The Selective Service System, or the draft, was another critical component of the government's wartime measures. Instituted in 1940, it required all men aged 21 to 45 to register for military service. This system ensured a steady flow of soldiers to the front lines, but it also stirred controversy and resistance. Conscientious objectors, many of them religious pacifists, faced imprisonment or were assigned to non-combat roles. The draft highlighted the tension between individual beliefs and national duty.

In the midst of these sweeping changes, the judiciary played its part. The Supreme Court, led by Chief Justice Harlan F. Stone, upheld many of the government's wartime actions, though not without dissent. Landmark cases like Korematsu v. United States, which justified the internment of Japanese Americans, sparked intense debate about the balance between security and liberty.

These decisions had far-reaching implications, shaping the legal landscape of civil rights and national security.

The government's wartime measures were a mosaic of initiatives, each addressing different facets of the nation's needs. From economic policies to security protocols, each measure was a piece of the larger strategy to preserve democracy and secure victory. These actions were not without their controversies and consequences, but they underscored the government's commitment to navigating the treacherous waters of war with resolve and ingenuity. The legacy of these measures, a testament to the complexity and urgency of wartime governance, continues to inform the nation's approach to security and liberty in the face

of new challenges.

CHAPTER 4: CRITICAL BATTLES

The Battle of Britain began in the summer of 1940, when the skies over England buzzed with the drone of German bombers. The Luftwaffe, led by Hermann Göring, sought to crush the Royal Air Force (RAF) and pave the way for an invasion. British pilots, many barely out of their teens, took to the air in

Spitfires and Hurricanes. They faced staggering odds, yet their resolve never wavered. Radar technology gave the RAF a crucial edge, allowing them to detect incoming raids and scramble fighters with precision. The Luftwaffe's relentless assault aimed to break British morale by targeting both military and civilian infrastructure. Night after night, Londoners huddled in underground shelters as bombs rained down. Yet, the Blitz, as it came to be known, only steeled the nation's resolve. Prime Minister Winston Churchill's stirring speeches galvanised the public, famously declaring, "Never in the field of human conflict was so much owed by so many to so few."

Meanwhile, across the vast expanse of North Africa, the desert became the stage for a different kind of warfare. The Battle of El Alamein in 1942 marked a turning point. General Bernard Montgomery, or "Monty" as his troops affectionately called him, led the British Eighth Army against the formidable Afrika Korps commanded by Field Marshal Erwin Rommel, the "Desert Fox." The terrain was unforgiving, with scorching days and freezing nights, but Montgomery's meticulous planning and the arrival of fresh American supplies tipped the balance. The Allies' victory at El Alamein halted the Axis advance towards the Suez Canal, a vital lifeline for British shipping.

On the Eastern Front, the Battle of Stalingrad raged with unparalleled ferocity. Soviet forces, under the command of Generals Zhukov and Chuikov, fought tooth and nail to defend the city bearing Stalin's name. The Germans, led by Field Marshal Friedrich Paulus, had captured much of the city by the autumn of 1942. However, the Soviet strategy of drawing the Germans into brutal urban combat sapped the enemy's strength. The Red Army encircled Paulus's forces in a daring counteroffensive, Operation Uranus. Trapped and starving in the freezing winter, the German

Sixth Army was forced to surrender in February 1943. Stalingrad was a catastrophic defeat for Hitler and marked the beginning of the Soviet Union's westward push.

In the Pacific Theatre, the Battle of Midway in June 1942 was a defining moment. Admiral Chester W. Nimitz, using intelligence gleaned from codebreakers, anticipated

Japanese Admiral Isoroku Yamamoto's plans. The Americans, despite being outnumbered, launched a daring preemptive strike. Their dive bombers inflicted devastating damage on the Japanese carriers Akagi, Kaga, and Soryu. This victory turned the tide in the Pacific, halting Japanese expansion and putting them on the defensive.

D-Day, 6th June 1944, saw the largest amphibious invasion in history. Operation Overlord was meticulously planned by General Dwight D. Eisenhower. The Allies landed on the beaches of Normandy, facing fierce German resistance. American forces stormed Omaha and Utah beaches, while British and Canadian troops landed on Gold, Juno, and Sword. The Mulberry harbours, prefabricated in Britain and towed across the Channel, played a crucial role in sustaining the invasion. Paratroopers dropped behind enemy lines, disrupting German communications and fortifications. The liberation of France began, and the Allies steadily advanced towards Germany.

The Battle of the Bulge in December 1944 was Hitler's last-ditch effort to turn the tide. German forces launched a surprise attack through the Ardennes, aiming to split the Allied lines and capture the vital port of Antwerp. The Allies, caught off guard, were pushed back, creating a "bulge" in the front lines. Yet, under General Patton's leadership, American forces regrouped and counterattacked, eventually repelling the Germans. The harsh winter conditions and the determination of Allied troops, including the famous stand at Bastogne, thwarted Hitler's plans.

The war in the Pacific culminated in the Battle of Okinawa in April 1945. This bloody conflict saw ferocious fighting as American forces sought to capture the island, a strategic point for launching an invasion of Japan. The Japanese defenders, entrenched in fortified positions, fought with grim determination. Kamikaze pilots launched suicide attacks on the American fleet, causing significant damage. Despite the high cost in lives, the Allies secured Okinawa, bringing them within striking distance of the Japanese mainland.

The battles were as varied as the terrains on which they were fought, each demanding unique strategies and sheer tenacity. The relentless push from both the Eastern and Western fronts forced Germany into a desperate defense. By April 1945, Soviet forces had encircled Berlin. The final assault saw fierce street-by-street fighting, as Hitler's once-vaunted Wehrmacht crumbled under the weight of the Allied onslaught. On 30th April, Hitler took his own life, and on 8th May, Germany surrendered unconditionally.

In the Pacific, the atomic bombings of Hiroshima and Nagasaki in August 1945 by American forces brought a devastating end to the war. The sheer destructive power of the bombs forced Japan to surrender on 15th August, ending the deadliest conflict in human history. These critical battles shaped the course of the Second World War, each a testament to strategy, courage, and sacrifice. The Allies, through coordination and determination, overcame the formidable Axis powers, securing a hard-fought victory and shaping the post-war world.

CHAPTER 5: PUBLIC PERCEPTION AND MEDIA

During World War II, the role of the media in shaping public perception was immense. Newspapers, radio broadcasts, films, and posters were the primary means of communication. They aimed to inform, inspire, and influence the populace, creating a unified front against the Axis powers. Journalists like Edward R. Murrow brought the war into American living rooms with his vivid reports from the bombed-out streets of London. His broadcasts, starting with "This is London," captured the resilience of the British people, forging a deep connection with American listeners and bolstering support for the Allies.

Hollywood became a powerful propaganda tool. The Office of War Information (OWI) collaborated with filmmakers to produce movies that portrayed the war effort positively. Films like "Casablanca" and "Mrs. Miniver" highlighted themes of sacrifice, duty, and patriotism. These movies were more than entertainment; they were designed to boost morale and reinforce the idea that the war was a fight for freedom and democracy.

Radio was another crucial medium. Programs like "Fibber McGee and Molly" and "The Jack Benny Program" incorporated war themes into their comedy sketches, subtly reinforcing the message of unity and perseverance. President Franklin D. Roosevelt's fireside chats also played a significant role. His calm, reassuring voice provided a sense of stability and direction, making complex war strategies understandable to the average American.

Print media, including newspapers and magazines, played a vital role in disseminating information and shaping opinions. War correspondents like Ernie Pyle provided firsthand accounts from the front lines. Pyle's columns, which focused on the daily lives and struggles of ordinary soldiers, humanised the war and made it relatable to the public. His stories of bravery and camaraderie resonated deeply, fostering a sense of solidarity and pride.

Propaganda posters were ubiquitous, urging citizens to buy war bonds, conserve resources, and support the troops. Iconic images like Rosie the Riveter symbolised the crucial role of women in the workforce. Slogans like "Loose Lips Sink Ships" emphasised the importance of discretion and vigilance. These visual campaigns were not just about disseminating information; they were about creating a culture of participation and responsibility.

The government was acutely aware of the power of media in controlling the narrative. The OWI's Bureau of Motion Pictures reviewed and approved scripts, ensuring that films aligned with wartime objectives. The Office of Censorship monitored communications, preventing sensitive information from reaching the enemy. This control extended to international media as well. The Voice of America, established in 1942, broadcast news and information to occupied Europe, countering Axis propaganda and providing a lifeline of truth to those living under oppressive regimes.

However, not all media was blindly supportive. Publications like the Chicago Tribune and individuals like Charles Lindbergh voiced isolationist sentiments, arguing against U.S.

involvement in the war. These voices represented a significant minority that believed America's resources should be focused on domestic issues rather than foreign entanglements. Despite this, the overwhelming majority of media outlets rallied behind the war effort, recognising the existential threat posed by the Axis powers.

War photography brought the brutal reality of conflict into stark relief. Images from the front lines, like those taken by Robert Capa during the D-Day landings, captured the harrowing experiences of soldiers in a way words could not. These photographs were published in magazines like Life and Time, providing the public with a visceral understanding of the sacrifices being made. They served as a powerful reminder of the stakes of the conflict and the necessity of unwavering support.

The media also played a role in highlighting the contributions of minority groups. Stories of the Tuskegee Airmen, an all-Black squadron of fighter pilots, and the Navajo Code Talkers, who used their native language to create an unbreakable code, were celebrated. These narratives helped challenge prevailing prejudices and demonstrated the diverse contributions to the war effort.

Public perception was further shaped by the portrayal of enemy leaders. Figures like Hitler, Mussolini, and Hirohito were depicted as monstrous tyrants. Cartoons by artists like Dr. Seuss and propaganda films by directors like Frank Capra's "Why

We Fight" series portrayed the Axis powers as evil incarnate, making the moral imperative of the war clear.

The media's influence extended beyond the war's end. Post-war, newsreels and documentaries chronicled the liberation of concentration camps, revealing the full horror of the Holocaust. These images were shocking and deeply impactful, ensuring that the atrocities committed by the Nazis were etched into the public consciousness. They reinforced the righteousness of the Allied cause and the importance of vigilance against tyranny.

The relationship between the government and the media during WWII was complex, characterised by cooperation, control, and occasionally conflict. While the government sought to guide the narrative to support the war effort, journalists and filmmakers balanced the need for truthful reporting with patriotic duty. This partnership was instrumental in maintaining public morale and ensuring widespread support for the war.

The legacy of wartime media is profound. It demonstrated the power of communication in shaping public opinion and mobilising a nation. The techniques and strategies developed during this period set the stage for modern propaganda and public relations. The lessons learned about the importance of transparency, the need for accurate reporting, and the impact of media on national unity continue to resonate in today's information landscape.

CHAPTER 6:
INTERNATIONAL CONTEXT

Throughout the World War II, the global stage was a complex web of alliances, conflicts, and political maneuvering. Nations across continents were embroiled in a struggle that transcended borders, ideologies, and cultures. The international context of the war shaped its course, influencing strategies, outcomes, and the post-war world.

The Axis powers, led by Germany, Italy, and Japan, sought to expand their territories through military conquest. Germany, under Adolf Hitler, pursued a policy of Lebensraum, aiming to create a vast empire in Eastern Europe. The Nazi invasion of Poland in 1939 triggered the war, prompting Britain and France to declare war on Germany. Italy, led by Benito Mussolini, sought to recreate the glory of the Roman Empire, launching invasions in Africa and the Balkans. Japan, driven by the need for resources, embarked on a campaign of expansion in Asia, invading China and later attacking Southeast Asia and the Pacific.

The Allies, a coalition of nations opposed to the Axis, included major powers like the United States, the Soviet Union, and Britain, along with numerous other countries. The alliance was not without its tensions. The Soviet Union, led by Joseph Stalin, had initially signed a non-aggression pact with Germany, allowing Hitler to focus on Western Europe. This pact ended abruptly in 1941 when Germany invaded the Soviet Union. The United States, under President Franklin D. Roosevelt, provided crucial support to the Allies through the Lend-Lease program before officially entering the war after the Japanese attack on Pearl Harbor in December 1941.

Europe was the primary theatre of war, with battles raging from the Western Front to the Eastern

Front. The Blitzkrieg, or lightning war, tactics employed by Germany in the early years brought rapid victories in Poland, France, and the Low Countries. However, the tide turned with significant battles such as Stalingrad and El Alamein, where the Allies began to push back. The D-Day landings in Normandy in June 1944 marked the beginning of the end for Nazi Germany, leading to the liberation of Western Europe and the eventual fall of Berlin in May 1945.

In the Pacific, the war was characterized by island-hopping campaigns and brutal naval battles. The Battle of Midway in 1942 was a turning point, with the United States inflicting a decisive defeat on the Japanese fleet. The capture of Iwo Jima and Okinawa brought American forces closer to Japan, culminating in the dropping of atomic bombs on Hiroshima and Nagasaki in August 1945. Japan's surrender followed shortly after, bringing an end to the war.

The war also had profound effects on colonies and occupied territories. In Africa, Asian, and the Middle East, colonial subjects were drawn into the conflict, serving in military forces or supporting war efforts through labor and resources. The war's end saw a wave of decolonization, as former colonies sought independence, inspired by the principles of self-determination and emboldened by the weakening of European powers.

Diplomatically, the war reshaped international relations. The Yalta and Potsdam conferences, attended by the leaders of the United States, the Soviet Union, and Britain, laid the groundwork for the post-war order. The United Nations was established in 1945, aiming to prevent future conflicts and promote international cooperation. However, the wartime alliance between the Soviet Union and the Western Allies quickly fractured, giving rise to the Cold War. The ideological divide between communism and capitalism dominated global politics for the next four decades.

Economic factors played a significant role in the war. The Axis powers sought to secure resources through conquest, while the Allies leveraged their industrial capacity and economic cooperation. The United States, in particular, became the arsenal of democracy, supplying vast quantities of arms, vehicles, and supplies to its allies. The war effort spurred technological innovation and industrial growth, laying the foundation for post-war economic booms in the United States and other Allied nations.

Propaganda was a powerful tool used by all sides to shape public perception and maintain morale. The Allies promoted themes of freedom, justice, and unity, while the Axis powers used propaganda to justify their expansionist goals and vilify their enemies. Films, radio broadcasts, posters, and literature were all employed to influence opinion and garner support for the war effort.

The human cost of the war was staggering. Tens of millions of soldiers and civilians lost their lives, with the Holocaust standing as a stark reminder of the atrocities committed. The war's end brought about significant social changes, including the movement for civil rights in the United States and the push for gender equality, as women who had entered the workforce during the war sought to retain their newfound roles.

In Asia, the end of the war saw the beginning of significant political upheaval. The Chinese Civil War resumed between the Nationalists and Communists, leading to the establishment of the People's Republic of China in 1949. In India, the struggle for independence from British rule gained momentum, culminating in independence in 1947. The partition of India and Pakistan was marked by widespread violence and mass migrations, setting the stage for future conflicts in the region.

Europe faced the daunting task of reconstruction. The Marshall Plan, initiated by the United States, provided substantial financial aid to Western European countries to rebuild their economies and prevent the spread of communism. Eastern Europe, meanwhile, fell under Soviet influence, leading to the establishment of communist governments and the division of Germany into East and West.

The war's legacy continues to shape international relations and global politics. The lessons learned about the dangers of totalitarianism, the importance of international cooperation, and the need for vigilance against aggression remain relevant. The memory of the war serves as a reminder of the human capacity for both destruction and resilience, and the ongoing quest for peace and justice in the international arena.

CHAPTER 7: LONG-TERM IMPACT

World War II left a profound impact on the world, reshaping politics, economics, and societies for decades. The geopolitical landscape saw a dramatic shift. The war led to the emergence of the United States and the Soviet Union as superpowers, setting the stage for the Cold War. This ideological conflict between capitalism and communism influenced global politics for nearly half a century, creating a bipolar world divided into spheres of influence. The iron curtain descended across Europe, splitting the continent into democratic and communist blocs.

The economic repercussions were equally significant. The

Marshall Plan, initiated by the United States, aimed to rebuild war-torn Europe, providing over $12 billion in aid. This plan not only helped revive European economies but also fostered closer economic ties between the United States and Western Europe, laying the foundation for the modern transatlantic alliance. Meanwhile, the Soviet Union established its own economic sphere, binding

Eastern European countries into the Council for Mutual Economic Assistance (Comecon).

World War II accelerated decolonization. European powers, weakened by the war, faced growing demands for independence from their colonies. In Asia, India gained independence from Britain in 1947, followed by numerous other countries. In Africa, the

1950s and 1960s saw a wave of decolonization, with nations like Ghana, Nigeria, and Kenya gaining independence. These new nations often faced significant challenges, including establishing stable governments and developing their economies, but their emergence marked the end of European imperial dominance.

The war also brought about significant social changes. In the United States, the return of millions of servicemen spurred economic growth and the development of the middle class. The G.I. Bill provided veterans with education and housing benefits, contributing to the post-war economic boom. However, it also highlighted racial inequalities, as many African American veterans faced discrimination and were denied the full benefits of the G.I. Bill, fueling the civil rights movement.

Women's roles changed dramatically due to the war. With men off fighting, women took on jobs traditionally held by men, working in factories, shipyards, and offices. This shift challenged traditional gender roles and laid the groundwork for the women's liberation movement in the

1960s and 1970s. Although many women returned to domestic roles after the war, the experience broadened their horizons and aspirations, leading to greater demands for equality and opportunities in the workforce.

Technological advancements during the war had long-lasting effects. The development of radar, jet engines, and nuclear technology revolutionized military capabilities. The atomic bombings of Hiroshima and Nagasaki not only ended the war with Japan but also ushered in the nuclear age. The subsequent arms race between the United States and the Soviet Union led to the development of increasingly powerful nuclear weapons and delivery systems, posing a constant threat of global annihilation during the Cold War.

The establishment of the United Nations in 1945 aimed to prevent future conflicts and promote international cooperation. The UN provided a platform for diplomacy and conflict resolution, although its effectiveness varied. The creation of institutions like the International Monetary Fund

(IMF) and the World Bank sought to stabilize the global economy and promote development, reflecting lessons learned from the economic turmoil of the interwar period.

The Holocaust, the systematic extermination of six million Jews by the Nazis, had a profound impact on global consciousness. The sheer scale of the atrocity led to a reevaluation of human rights and the necessity of preventing genocide. The Nuremberg Trials held Nazi leaders accountable for war crimes and crimes against humanity, establishing a precedent for international justice. The horror of the Holocaust also played a significant role in the establishment of the state of Israel in 1948, providing a homeland for Jewish survivors and refugees.

The cultural impact of World War II was immense. The war influenced literature, film, and art, reflecting the trauma and heroism of the period. Novels like "Catch-22" by Joseph Heller and "Slaughterhouse-Five" by Kurt Vonnegut captured the absurdity and brutality of war. Films such as "Saving Private

Ryan" and "Schindler's List" brought the experiences of soldiers and Holocaust victims to a new generation, ensuring that the lessons of the war were not forgotten.

The war also prompted significant advancements in medicine and science. The need to treat wounded soldiers led to developments in surgery, antibiotics, and blood transfusions. The urgency of wartime research accelerated scientific progress, leading to breakthroughs in fields like rocketry and computing. The wartime collaboration between scientists in the Manhattan Project laid the foundation for the post-war expansion of scientific research and the eventual space race.

World War II also had a lasting impact on national identities and collective memories. In the United States, the war fostered a sense of unity and purpose, contributing to the concept of the "Greatest Generation." In Europe, the devastation of the war and the subsequent recovery efforts strengthened the drive towards European integration, leading to the formation of the European

Union. In Japan and Germany, the war left deep scars, prompting reflections on militarism and leading to pacifist policies in the post-war period.

The legacy of World War II continues to shape the world. The lessons learned about the dangers of totalitarianism, the importance of international cooperation, and the need for vigilance against aggression remain relevant. The war's impact on technology, society, and global politics continues to influence the present, reminding us of the profound consequences of conflict and the enduring pursuit of peace and justice.

CONCLUSION

World War II's impact stretches far beyond the battlefield. This massive conflict reshaped nations, economies, and societies in ways that continue to reverberate today. The war propelled the United States and the Soviet Union into superpower status, setting the stage for the Cold War. This bipolar world divided nations into Western and Eastern blocs, fueling decades of ideological, political, and military tension.

Economically, the war spurred innovation and growth. The Marshall Plan, a bold U.S. initiative, rebuilt Europe's shattered economies, fostering unprecedented transatlantic cooperation. The Soviet Union, meanwhile, tightened its grip on Eastern Europe, creating a stark economic and political divide. This division set the scene for the Iron Curtain and the ensuing struggle between democracy and communism.

Decolonization was another significant outcome. European powers, exhausted and financially drained, couldn't maintain their colonies. Countries in Asia and Africa seized the moment, pushing for independence. India, Ghana, Nigeria, and others broke free from colonial rule, although they faced immense challenges in building new nations. These newly independent states had to navigate the complex geopolitics of the Cold War while striving for economic stability and social cohesion.

On the home front, societal shifts were profound. In the U.S., the G.I. Bill provided veterans with education and home loans, fueling a post-war economic boom and expanding the middle class. However, this also highlighted racial disparities as African American veterans often faced discrimination, sparking the civil rights movement. Women, who had entered the workforce in droves during the war, began demanding equal opportunities, laying the groundwork for the feminist movements of the 1960s and 1970s.

Technological advancements during the war were monumental. Radar, jet engines, and nuclear technology revolutionized both military and civilian life. The atomic bomb, while devastating, led to nuclear power and medicine. The wartime collaboration among scientists, particularly the Manhattan Project, laid the foundation for post-war scientific research and the space race, leading to technological leaps in various fields.

The formation of the United Nations marked a significant step toward global governance. Aimed at preventing future conflicts, the UN became a platform for diplomacy and international cooperation. It played a crucial role in decolonization, human rights advocacy, and conflict resolution. Institutions like the IMF and World Bank were also established to stabilize the global economy and promote development, reflecting lessons learned from the economic turmoil that preceded and followed the war.

The Holocaust, the genocide of six million Jews, left an indelible mark on human history. This atrocity led to a global reckoning with the horrors of genocide and the necessity of human rights protections. The Nuremberg Trials set a precedent for international law, holding leaders accountable for war crimes and crimes against humanity. The creation of Israel in 1948 provided a homeland for Jewish survivors and refugees, though it also set the stage for ongoing conflict in the Middle East.

Cultural impacts of the war were vast. Literature, film, and art reflected the trauma and heroism of the period. Works like "Catch-22" and "Slaughterhouse-Five" explored the absurdity and brutality of war, while films like "Saving Private Ryan" and "Schindler's List" brought these experiences to new generations. These cultural artifacts ensure that the lessons of World War II remain in the public consciousness.

Medicine and science saw rapid advancements. Wartime needs led to improvements in surgery, antibiotics, and blood transfusions. The urgency of war research accelerated progress in rocketry and computing, laying the groundwork for post-war innovations and the eventual space race. The collaboration among scientists during the war led to a boom in post-war scientific research, significantly impacting technology and medicine.

The war also left lasting scars on national identities. In the United

States, it fostered a sense of unity and purpose, contributing to the "Greatest Generation" narrative. In Europe, the devastation and subsequent recovery efforts strengthened the drive toward European integration, leading to the formation of the European Union. For Japan and Germany, the war prompted deep reflections on militarism, leading to pacifist policies and democratic reforms in the post-war period.

The legacy of World War II is evident in today's geopolitical and social landscapes. The lessons learned about the dangers of totalitarianism, the value of international cooperation, and the importance of human rights continue to guide global policies. The war's impact on technology, society, and global politics underscores the profound consequences of conflict and the enduring pursuit of peace and justice.

The global power dynamics shifted dramatically. The Cold War, spurred by the ideological battle between the U.S. and the Soviet Union, influenced international relations for decades. This period saw numerous proxy wars, nuclear arms races, and political maneuvers, as both superpowers vied for influence around the world. The legacy of this struggle is still felt today, shaping modern geopolitics and international relations.

World War II also transformed everyday life. Technological innovations like radar, jet engines, and nuclear power, developed for the war, found peacetime applications that revolutionized industries and daily living. The rise of consumer culture, driven by economic prosperity and technological advancements, reshaped societal norms and lifestyles.

Women's roles in society underwent significant changes. The war had drawn millions of women into the workforce, challenging traditional gender roles. Post-war, many women sought to maintain their newfound independence and continue working, leading to shifts in family dynamics and the labor market. These changes laid the groundwork for the feminist movements of the 1960s and beyond, pushing for greater gender equality and rights.

In the international sphere, the establishment of the United

Nations marked a new era of diplomacy and cooperation. The UN aimed to prevent future conflicts, promote human rights, and support economic development. Although its effectiveness has varied, the UN remains a central player in global governance. Institutions like the IMF and World Bank, created in the war's aftermath, have played key roles in stabilizing the global economy and supporting development efforts.

The war's cultural impact remains significant. The experiences of World War II have been immortalized in countless books, films, and artworks, ensuring that the lessons and memories of the conflict endure. These cultural representations help to keep the history and impact of the war alive in public consciousness, providing important reflections on the human experience and the costs of conflict.

World War II fundamentally reshaped the world. The political, economic, and social changes set in motion by the war continue to influence global dynamics. The conflict's legacy is a testament to the profound and lasting impact of such a monumental event in human history.

9 798227 228468